SPACE OBSERVER

The Planets

by
Jenny Tesar

Heinemann Library
Chicago, Illinois

Customer Service 888-454-2279
Visit our website at www.heinemannlibrary.com

ISBN 1-57572-580-0

Library of Congress Cataloging-in-Publication Data

Tesar, Jenny E.
  The Planets/ by Jenny Tesar.
      p.   cm. — (Space Observer)
  Includes bibliographical references and index.
Summary: Introduces the planets of the solar system, discussing the location, size, and climate of each.
  ISBN 0-8050-4477-9 (lib. bdg.)
   1.Planets—Juvenile Literature. [1. Planets]. I. Title.
  II. Series: Tesar, Jenny E. Space observer
  QB602.T47   1997
  523.4—dc21   97-25179
                                                              CIP
                                                               AC

Acknowledgments
The author and publishers are grateful to the following for permission to reproduce copyright photographs:
Pages 4-5: ©Blackbirch Press, Inc.; pages 6, 18, 22-23: ©NASA/Science Source/Photo Researchers, Inc.; page 7: A.S.P./Science Source/Photo Researchers, Inc.; pages 8-9, 14: ©Julian Baum/Science Photo Library/Photo Researchers, Inc.; page 10: ©John Foster/Science Source/Photo Researchers, Inc.; page 11: Gazelle Technologies, Inc.; page 12: U.S. Geological Survey/Science Photo Library/Photo Researchers, Inc.; pages 13, 16, 19: ©NASA; page 15: A. Gragera, Latin Stock/Science Photo Library/Photo Researchers, Inc.; page 17: ©NASA/Peter Arnold, Inc.; pages 20, 21: ©W. Kaufmann/JPL/SS/Photo Researchers, Inc.

Cover photograph: NASA/Peter Arnold, Inc.

Every effort has been made to contact copyright holders of any material reproduced in this book. Any omissions will be rectified in subsequent printings if notice is given to the publisher.

Some words are shown in bold, **like this**. You can find out what they mean by looking in the glossary.

Printed by South China Printing in Hong Kong / China

Contents

The Solar System

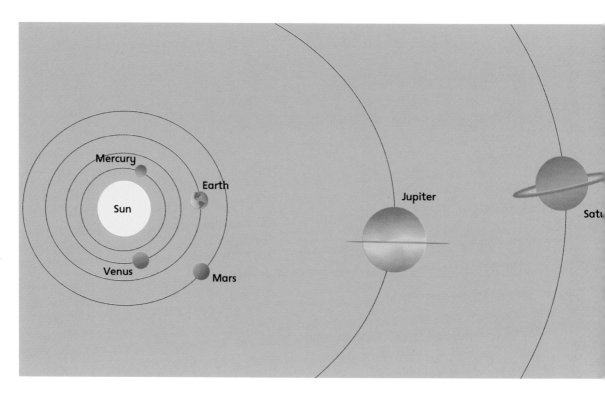

Our solar system has nine planets, including Earth.

Our Earth is part of the Solar System. Solar means sun. The Sun is the center of our Solar System. The Sun is a huge star.

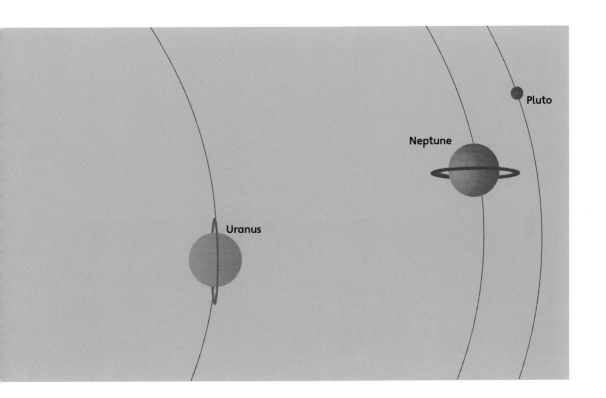

Nine round (ball-shaped) **planets** move in paths called **orbits.** These are like giant circles around the sun. Scientists send **probes** to some of the planets to learn more about the Solar System.

Mercury

Distance from Sun: 36 million miles
Number of Moons: 0
Relative Size: Eighth largest

Mercury is the closest **planet** to the Sun.
Because Mercury is so close to the Sun, the
side that faces the Sun gets very hot. That
side is much hotter than any place on Earth.

Mercury is closest to the Sun.

Mercury's **surface** looks like our Moon.

Mariner 10 was a probe that visited Mercury. It took hundreds of pictures. The pictures showed that Mercury looks a lot like our Moon.

Venus

Distance from Sun: 67 million miles
Number of Moons: 0
Relative Size: Sixth largest

Venus is the second **planet** from the Sun. It is the closest planet to Earth.

Venus and Earth are about the same size. But thick **acid** clouds always cover Venus. People, animals, and plants from Earth couldn't live in this **atmosphere.**

More than 20 **probes** have visited Venus.

An artist's picture of one of 20 probes that have visited Venus.

Earth

Distance from Sun: 93 million miles
Number of Moons: 1
Relative Size: Fifth largest

Earth is the third **planet** from the Sun. Earth has one **moon.** The moon travels around Earth—at the same time that Earth travels around the Sun.

The moon is always circling around Earth.

Almost three-quarters of Earth's surface is covered with water.

Earth is the only planet with water on its
surface. It is the only planet on which life
is known.

Mars

Distance from Sun: 142 million miles
Number of Moons: 2
Relative Size: Seventh largest

Mars is the fourth **planet** from the Sun. It is about half the size of Earth. It has a red color.

Mars is known for its red color.

Mars has large craters shaped like bowls.

Millions of years ago, Mars had water. Today, it is dry. Many scientists think there once was life on Mars. Maybe tiny living things are there today. Two **probes** that arrived in 1997 looked at Mars for signs of life.

Jupiter

Distance from Sun: 484 million miles
Number of Moons: 16 or more
Relative Size: Largest

Jupiter is the fifth **planet** from the Sun. You could put all the other planets inside Jupiter and still have extra room!

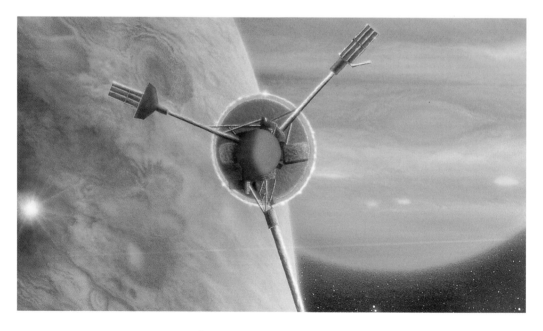

An artist's picture of a probe passing a **moon** on its way to Jupiter.

An artist's picture shows Jupiter's rings and some of its moons.

Jupiter is not solid like Earth. It is a huge ball of **gases.**

Six **probes** have already visited Jupiter. They discovered thin rings that circle the planet. Scientists think the rings are made of rocks.

Saturn

Distance from Sun: 886 million miles
Number of Moons: 20 or more
Relative Size: Second largest

Saturn is the sixth **planet** from the Sun.
Like Jupiter, it is a giant ball of **gases.**

Saturn is famous for the beautiful rings
that circle it. The rings are large and flat.

Saturn's rings are made of ice and dust.

A collage showing Saturn and some of its many moons.

They are made of billions of small pieces of ice and dust. Saturn has more **moons** than any other planet. Three **probes** have visited Saturn.

Uranus

Distance from the Sun: 1.7 billion miles
Number of Moons: 15 or more
Relative Size: Third largest

Uranus is the seventh planet from the Sun.
It is a **gas planet,** like Jupiter and Saturn.
Like the other gas planets, Uranus has rings.
They are very dark.

An artist's picture of Uranus, a gas planet with dark rings.

An artist's picture shows *Voyager 2* visiting Uranus.

Voyager 2 was the only **probe** to visit Uranus. It arrived there in 1986, after visiting Jupiter and Saturn.

Neptune

Distance from Sun: 2.8 billion miles
Number of Moons: 8 or more
Relative Size: Fourth largest

Neptune is usually the eighth **planet** from the Sun. But because of its **orbit,** sometimes Pluto is closer to the Sun than Neptune.

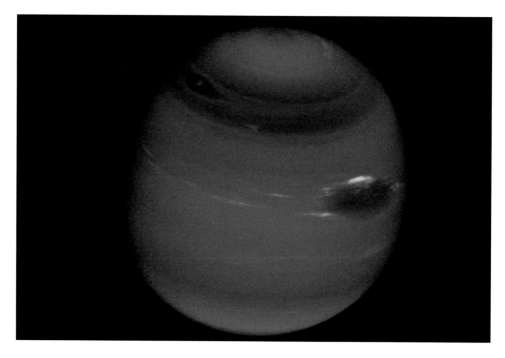

Neptune's rings are too thin to show in this photo.

Icy Triton is the largest of Neptune's moons.

Neptune is a **gas** planet and has rings. This planet also has at least eight **moons.** The biggest is Triton. Almost half of Triton is covered with ice. It even has ice volcanoes!

In 1989, *Voyager 2* became the first **probe** to visit Neptune.

Pluto

Distance from Sun: 3.6 billion miles
Number of Moons: 1
Relative Size: Smallest

Pluto travels in an unusual **orbit** around the Sun. Usually, Pluto is the farthest **planet** from the Sun. But sometimes its path crosses Neptune's path. Then Pluto is closer to the Sun—and Neptune is the farthest planet.

Pluto is a rocky planet, not a **gas** planet. It is very cold. Very little of the Sun's heat reaches Pluto.

An artist's drawing shows Pluto and the **moon** called Charon that circles around it.

Glossary

acid strong substance that can burn your skin

atmosphere layer of **gases** around a planet

gases substances that spread to fill a space

moon ball-shaped object that circles a planet

orbit path around the Sun or around another object in space

planet one of nine huge, ball-shaped objects that circle the sun

probes vehicles without people that are sent to space so that scientists can learn more

surface outside layer of something

More Books to Read

Fowler, Alan. *The Sun's Family of Planets.* Danbury, Conn.: Children's Press, 1993.

Fradin, Dennis B. *Saturn.* Danbury, Conn.: Children's Press, 1993.

Ride, Sally. *Voyager: An Adventure to the Edge of the Solar System.* New York: Crown Books for Young Readers, 1992.

Robinson, Fay. *Space Probes to the Planets.* Morton Grove, Ill.: Albert Whitman & Company 1993.

Index